Black. Don't. Crack.

POEMS ABOUT BLACKNESS & MENTAL HEALTH

KAREN MUTSATSA

OTHER POETRY COLLECTIONS

BY KAREN MUTSATSA

The human condition is conditioned:

Poems on humanity.

Thought Daughter:

My miscellaneous, candid, & dark(est) poems.

Sad Girl Poetry:

Poems about my girlhood.

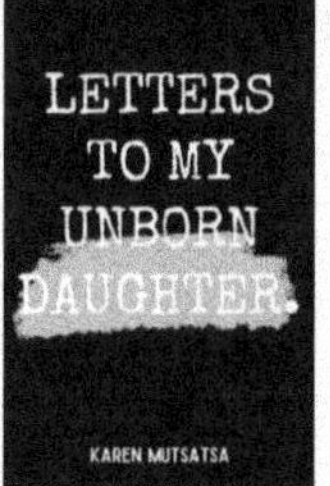

Letters to my unborn daughter:

10 poems to my unborn girlchild.

Hate to love:

Poems about rising & falling in love.

Cripple - poems on how the world tried to make me hate myself:

Poems on being disabled.

Metaphysics - mumbo jumbo poetry:

Existential poetry.

Dreams & Drugs - It's complicated:

Poems on ambition & addiction.

CONTENTS

Preface

I've never understood racism. I think it is mean, evil, and unfair. As stated in my poem 'Refugee' (page 57), I first learned of my otherness when I arrived in Britain. In Africa, not only were most people black, but most Zimbabweans revered white/British society anyway, so it was the norm to aspire towards whiteness e.g., speaking good English. Hating white people never crossed my mind, I never thought about their features or how different they were to me. I just saw people. Yet, as a five-year-old in 2002 Britain, I learned that my nose was 'flat' and my lips were big for the first time: according to another student. I learned that it was popular to disrespect darker skinned people within black communities, e.g., through slang like 'blick', and to disrespect the diaspora, e.g., 'fresh off the boat'. In 2002 Britain, I learned that a lot of Caribbean people felt superior to Africans (xenophobia), and that a lot of South Asian people felt superior to all black people.

Slowly and surely, I learned that whiteness was 'The Standard', and that all other shades of the human spectrum fell beneath it accordingly, in hierarchy of pigment. In worst cases, people seperated themselves in accordance to continents, countries, and counties - even postcodes! That's why it is interesting to see just how ideas have changed in my lifetime, within and outside of blackness. How Afrobeat and Amapiano are being popularised globally, even by black America, meanwhile, I grew up hearing black American slurs towards Africans like "African booty scratcher".

I mention all of this because that is what this collection of poems is about: radical ethnicity-related accountability and authenticity. In this collection, I speak of the wrongs that have been imposed upon me by whiteness, but I also speak of the wrongs I've experienced within my own community.

Of course, I've made a lot of generalisations in this preface. I've grouped people for the sake of argument, but I am fully aware that life isn't black and white (pun intended). As indicated by the grey pages in this book, there is always a grey area. I am not a militant person, but I won't pretend in my art either, since I do enough of that in society. I've experienced love from all different kinds of people, but I've also experienced unimaginable and continuous injustice from specific people that are inside and outside of blackness. Lastly, this book's artwork is a homage to Jean-Michel Basquiat and Keith Haring.

With love, Gamu.

WHY ARE YOU SO ANGRY?

"Why are you so angry?"
Mama asked.

And I replied: "'Cos it's a fallacy
That they're not seeing me.
In the streets I bleed—
Fighting for my right to breathe.
You ask me why
But never how.
They know my name, won't say it loud,
Drenched in shame, this life of doubt,
I've screamed for years without a sound."

"But why are you so angry?"
Mama asked again.

And I replied: "Partly 'cos I'm loveless and I've lost the taste,
To fix what's broken in Pandora's case.
I've lied and cheated for no one's sake,
Made victims of the innocent... I feel ashamed.
With my fear and guilt keeping me awake,
There's a pistol by my side, I feel unsafe.
So maybe I'm not angry Mama... I'm just afraid."

About the poem:

Why are you so angry?

If you cannot be loved, feel wanted, and safe, is it better to be respected out of fear? If all you feel is that you're a trapped monster, and that any attempt at being heard or seen can, and has resulted in your further victimisation, wouldn't you opt to become the monster they claim? Wouldn't you pretend to be the bully instead of the bullied just for the sake of survival? Just to be able to call yourself a person and show up in society. Unfortunately, when 'playing pretend' sometimes we go native and forget that we're playing roles or we become these roles, leading to regretful behaviour and life events. Take Bashy's 'Sweet Boys Turned Sour' song, and many other rappers who have voiced the experiences and lifepaths of how good kids turn bad in a mad city (Kendrick Lamar).

Adding my own experience into this, and where I was writing from, well, I've been angry for most of my life. I've been angry at society, myself, family, and life. Mostly at society, and as such, I wear an 'angry face' or a standoffish face when I am out and about, simply to repel people from interacting with me and/or thinking I can be their victim. Anyone who doesn't know me might think that I am rude, and I probably am, but I am also afraid of human interaction. I want people to think I am tougher than I am, so that they leave me alone. It's a defence mechanism, and it sadly works. For which, isn't that true of many young, marginalised people? Do we not become contradictions, and caricatures of our pain? Since the world misunderstands us, we tend to become personifications of that misunderstanding.

AFRICAN CHILD

African child, yours is the rhythm that plays wild.
Ridiculed and objectified within crowds
So, your treasures remain unfound,
Waiting for you to be proud
Of the past that made your now.

But black boys are beasts, and on black girls we feast,
We mould these Kings and Queens to be anything but free.
It's within the culture, and they 'do it for the culture',
Colourism, Sexism, and Homophobia—
Anything that keeps us questioning as we get older.
Then how can we get bolder?
Unexamined truths that keep us lower.

And yet, my history says I'm heaven sent,
But my people deny its relevance.
They'd rather worship something else,
and ignore the power in themselves.

Your thoughts are magic
But you call it spells,
Yet therein lies a freedom that you've never felt.
Soulful redemption = ultimate health,
But these boys and girls find their worth in sexual wealth.

I know your doldrums; I know your hell,
I've been searching for identity as well.
But abandon lies in which you dwell,
And remember the joys that kept you from darker realms.
African child... remember (your)Self.

About the poem:

African Child

Here's the thing, it is so easy to dwell in victimhood, and if you're not careful, it'll seduce you into forfeiting a life of integrity. At what point does one take responsibility for their pain, as the only solution worth seeking? By this I am attempting to ask: when will we, as black people collectively take accountability for the perpetuation of our own pain, as the only conversation worth having, in a world where freedom and peace is not given but earned, taken, and made?

This poem is about the (inner) African child and finding our way back home (Beyonce). I believe that most of what adversely affects black communities has been derived from an oppressive and imperialist history, but we refuse to abandon what we know for the unknown. Black culture is heavily saturated and interwoven with foreign and anti-black norms, which I attribute our cyclical woes to. So much of who we are and what we believe is anti-black dogma, which is fine for the rest of the world to believe (sarcasm), but not for us to internalise. I find it unacceptable how we readily and easily accept other people's surnames as our own, other people's languages, religions, politics, philosophies, complexions, fashion, knowledge, etc. Further, how we've allowed ourselves to be divided, and therefor conquered.

EBONY

Oh Mama, I know why you fret,
Struggling to make more out of less.
Cleaning up mine and their mess,
Whilst your self-esteem is made to rest.

Dear Black woman, riddled with pain
From their piecing gaze of disdain.
I'm sorry Ms Baartman for your life lived in shame,
Their eyes hurt more than when they used to beat you with a cane.

The darker the berry, the sweeter the juice,
But I guess you just don't see this to be true.
Bleaching your skin...
Inherited habits of trying to fit in.

Is that why you weave your hair into pretence?
Insecure about the features you were blessed with,
While overwhelmed by the chaos that you've been left with.

About the poem:

Ebony

An old poem, so some of my ideas are now more informed e.g., regarding weaves! However, this poem is briefly touching on black women's issues regarding being oversexualised, overburdened by responsibility, and undervalued by self and society. I'm a big believer in accountability and that nobody is coming to save you, nor will an oppressor give you the tools to overthrow them, you've got to find them yourself. Black women need to address these issues amongst themselves.

BANTU PRINCESS

Madzimbabwe are houses of stone,
And Zimbabwe is the biggest of all.
Wonder why I'm cold in brick homes,
When I'm just a Queen: dethroned.

This is strength that's been imposed,
From ancestors that died unknown.
I walk with tribes, I'm not alone,
That say the right do fight, and the wrong atone.

So, when the time comes that I should go,
...I was African and proud – and made it known.

About the poem:

Bantu Princess

I am from southern Africa, Zimbabwe specifically, therefore, of Bantu ethnic origin. This poem is an ode to my roots. A space, a place, and a declaration of who I am and where I am from. Further, the poem speaks of how it feels to be uprooted from where you belong. As the poem suggests, you can feel lonely and cold in foreign lands.

ASANTE SANA, BABA NAMA!

Children of the diaspora know one thing,
Assimilation to a culture that invades thy being.
When Cogito Ergo Sum, says: "I think therefore I am",
But Ubuntu's where I'm from, saying: "I am because we are".

Community is in my veins but in the West, it's often shunned,
As we're shocked by selfish ways, that infiltrated mother tongues.
This 'freedom' has me numb, for I belong to self and none,
Thus, mental health is what becomes, the joke we tell be more fun.

Mental health is what becomes, a debt to daughters and our sons,
When culture shock is what's among, the reasons why we lose our young.

But don't take this to say that I'm blind to where I'm from;
A country where human rights are not seen as human norms.
Our parents gave up lives so that we might have our own,
Whilst we inherited the lies of where we actually belong.

When you've been uprooted from the ground that you should know,
It's harder to settle down, though it's the only way to grow.
So, we don't have a nationality – the world is our home,
We are wandering children that are destined to roam.

About the poem:

Asante Sana, Baba naMai

Title translation: *Thank you, mum and dad (Swahili)*

As a first-generation immigrant, I am eternally grateful for my parent's sacrifices. I think most children of immigrants and immigrant children can relate to the burden of responsibility to succeed, as a 'thank you' to our parents for their gift of a better life. Without getting into the politics as to why our countries became inhabitable in the first place, the politics of where we grew up is much more relevant to the wellbeing of first world ethnic minority young people. Everything from the lack of an 'ethnic psychology', the experience of dual cultures and languages, the racism and othering, the adultification, to the invalidation of our trauma by family members because they had it worse, contributes to our success or lack thereof.

I've never felt like I belong anywhere, culturally. I prefer to enjoy my worlds in solitude, where I can be British without a superiority complex and not Anglo-Saxon/Romano, and African without being wilfully ignorant and self-hating. As I grow older, I realise that like many people, I've been a victim of severe miseducation about every aspect of my identity, my history, and thus my worth. My African culture has gifted me with all my wisdom and artistry but refused to see these gifts in me because I was born female. My British culture gave me the gift of innovation and selfhood yet denounces my personhood or genius because I am one of the people that the West has historically and continues to define as subhuman or 'wrong'/bad/faulty/undesirable. In a nutshell, that's what this poem is about. Being stuck between two worlds, loving two worlds, and suffering the consequences of both worlds...silently.

PRoTEcT
BLAcK
WoMEN

I heard thick thighs save lives, and take away stress,
That's why Sarah Baartman spent her life in racist press.
Show me "the ways of the ebony enchantress",
With hips that move like Yondo Sister in a silk-press.

While I'm inspired by the African mess
That was Brenda Fassie, during Apartheid regrets,
I think of Angela Davis and what she possibly meant,
By telling us to change the things we cannot accept.

Maybe referring to the things that oppress,
A billion women taught how to act and to dress.
'Cause I thought Calypso Rose told you – give it a rest,
Leave me alone, I wasn't born just so that I'm possessed.

Still, gender roles were never something that I cared to address,
For a cripple is asexual – according to society's lens.
But a love like Alice Walker and Tracy Chapman would quench–
My need to see a black woman loved with some sense.

Therefore, I hope my girlchild pretends,
That Destiny's Child wasn't born with two cents.
Yes, I hope my black daughter protects
her power, that they see as a threat.

About the poem:
Protect Black Women

One of the most rock & roll things I've done is be a black woman proudly and loudly. It has not been easy, and I used to think that it's a 'me' problem, until I went on the internet, in the library, and out into the world. Everywhere I looked, whether it was in history books, on TV, in the art I consumed, in my family, I saw black women being forced and outcast into resilience. Resilience is literally one's ability to take a hit and keep getting up, which means black women are predominantly recognised for their ability to take a beating from society. Additionally, the myth of black women being inhumanely strong is malignant folklore that contributes to the hypervisibility and invisibility of the black woman.

Isn't she so difficult, demanding, with unmeetable standards? Who does she think she is? Why is she never smiling?

You know, one of the reasons I love Camus is because I came to realise the joke of it all. Existence, and playing my role, that is. Like, the way I have to heighten my voice, and keep a neutral robotic smile on my face to keep meetings flowing accordingly, just to ensure my colleagues or acquaintances don't think I am a serial killer. It is exhausting. Outside of my other identities, being a black woman alone, is exhausting, and a weird position to be in, where you can see society's hypocrisy in 4K.

As a black woman, I feel like this thing that is wanted and unwanted simultaneously by everyone. I am wanted for my mothering, my wisdom, my labour, my body, and my womb. I am also unwanted for all of those same reasons, and then some more. Nevertheless, this is a poem for me and other black women (including my unborn daughter), hence, I've included notable black women (to me) in this piece. I'd like to thank these women, my mother, history's black girlchildren and tomorrow's, for existing and being beautiful regardless.

Sarah Baartman, The Symone (Drag Queen), Yondo Sister, Brenda Fassie, Angela Davis, Calypso Rose, Alice Walker, Tracy Chapman, Destiny's Child.

THE BLACK WOMAN ARCHETYPE

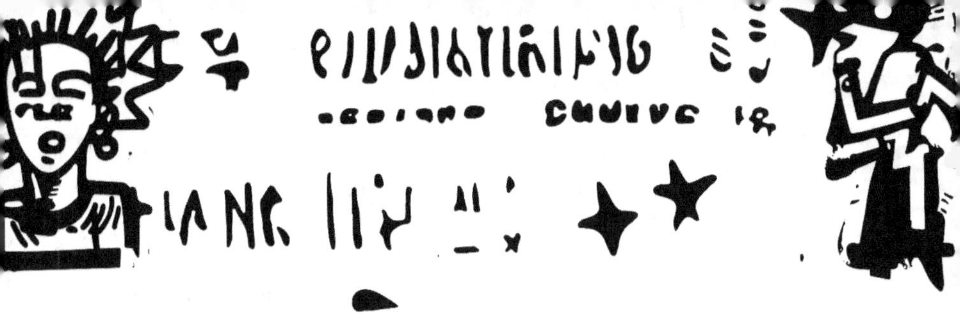

Mammy used to raise the white kids in the big house,
Whilst her own kids worked the fields and cried out.
Now Mammy works two jobs and drinks Grouse,
Still a slave with her kids just as lost and unfound.

She said it has been happening since HIStory.
"Black girl magic is a mystery—
That must be thwarted through misery!",
Cried the Voodoo sisters of Tituba's witchery.

Perhaps (it's because) they cannot believe it is not butter,
As Shea and Cocoa leave them with wonder.
This is Kente or Ankara, a whole spectrum of colour.
Head-wraps and verandas, Supermalt and Akaras.

But Mammy's babies then had babies,
and started bleaching, sew-ins and fake teeth.
'Brazilian Butt-Lift so they could love me',
Because Mammy's babies never had she.

About the poem:
The black woman archetype

This is a social commentary on my observation of what it means to be a black woman. At first, I started thinking about the black women I know, including myself and my mother, how we're often in two caregiving roles e.g., professionally, and personally. My carers, as a disabled person, who are often always black (and other people's carers too), as ethnic minority women comprise a significant proportion of the 'non/low-skilled' workforce. That is a book in itself, how we have created such a heartless world, through industrialisation and patriarchy, where jobs like caring for vulnerable people, teaching, medicine etc., all become less financially viable, with others even classified as non-skilled work. Granted, I have my grievance with the health and social care system, but it is broken because we are broken, because we stopped caring and valuing those who do. Anyway, back to how the people who facilitate my life, and the life of billions around the world, are the most abused by society. Outside of the care crisis, black women have been serving humanity for centuries. Whether it was through slavery or colonisation, as 'mammy' was also in Africa, and created through European colonisation, along with other 'low/non-skilled' jobs that were the very systems and practices which enabled capitalism to function.

Having said this, again, back to accountability. The poem then touches on some of what I consider maladaptive practices of black women, especially, self-hating or self-deprecating beauty fads that captivate young black people. I finish this piece by suggesting that black children/girls can be misled or start misbehaving because they saw and had so little of their mothers. This sentiment is deeper than suggested, as poverty and oppression have a nuanced way of sabotaging natural or adaptive growth. I didn't get to know my mother as well as I'd liked, or to the depths that my Western, white, UK-born peers could, as my mother was in survival mode all of my life. Getting to know her history or her person, was either potentially traumatic or considered trivial in comparison to the conversations that needed to be had. This is because black history, like my family's, is often inseparably associated with politically related adversity that any attempt to 'know' oneself or the ones you love, will inevitably lead you to pain and forgotten histories. Nevertheless, I dared to know my mother anyway, and I asked her about her life whenever I could. That's probably why I love my blackness and femininity so much, as I learned to love these aspects of myself through loving my mother and her story.

JIGABOO

Black man with your big-ass-dick,
No blood left for your brain, so you've got no wits.
And your daughter, never thought that she would grow so thick,
Like your mother, I've got something for her to lick.

"These bodies – unlike people – should be sold and whipped."
They weren't done, in today we're still sold and whipped.
I can't sleep with my people still unequipped–
With some knowledge, not the weapons that keep us eclipsed.

About the poem:

Jigaboo

Sometimes I play with shock value because I find pleasure in reminding society of its true face. Like, "hey, don't forget you created this word guys, and what it means!". This poem is designed to be uncomfortable, because it is describing topics and implicit attitudes that make black people feel uncomfortable all of the time. Even supposedly 'positive' stereotypes simply limit us to being objects for consumption and utility, as it was in the past. It seems, it has been a long popular cultural practice to disrespect black bodies, identities, and families. With black people themselves in on the joke, hence the ending of the poem. Which summarises that I am tired of black people fighting with weapons instead of knowledge/strategy.

KING/QUEEN ALREADY

They don't see a Shaka Zulu,
They see a fruit-loop.

They don't see the Queen of Zazzau,
They tell her pipe down.

But they too can be us now,
We break our own crowns.

Yes, you too keep us housebound,
With all your self-doubt.

About the poem:

King/Queen already

Inspired by Beyonce's song, this poem is about how the world might see us, instead of who we are. Additionally, who we used to be, versus who we are now. Lastly, what we could be, versus what we choose to be. Regardless of race/ethnicity, I believe a person can be the best version of themselves when they start believing that they have a best version – and that version is attainable. But it starts with choosing to pursue such fantasies.

LOST & FOUND

Mama, what can I say that hasn't been said?

Of all the blood they say Jesus bled,
How many ancestors have died instead?

Oh, my beautiful African mess,
Why have we forsaken humanity's bed?

"Be the victory to my sacrifices", you said,
But children are forgetful, Don't let it get to your head.

Oh Mama, what can I say that hasn't been said...

About the poem:

Lost & Found

As is suggested in the poem, I am speechless about the state of African affairs. Despite this, it won't stop me caring, living authentically, and radically in love with myself. However, I cannot deny the heaviness of my chest and my head, an experience that I am sure is shared by anyone that is in love with their African roots and experiencing homesickness. It's weird, because I was raised in the UK, since I was 5 years old, and I have not been back since. My only connection with Zimbabwe is through the internet. Also, Britain has always reminded me (personally), those I love, and those that look like me that we do not belong and will never belong. The western guilt, plausible deniability, unfounded hatred etc., never cease, so you never cease to be reminded of your oddness. That's one of the reasons why I've struggled to fully assimilate, but one of many other reasons is that I love who I am and where I come from. I just wish our African leaders felt the same.

44

Family, society,
The evil deep inside of me.
On death, and life, and fantasy,
I write it all to find some peace.

Loving you, my soul to keep,
Drugs, and dreams, and nothing cheap.
The thoughts that make it hard to sleep,
The blood I bleed, the ghosts I see.

The waters, skies, plants, and trees,
Kids, beasts, my favourite beings.
Teasing you and sexy things,
All your wants I turn to needs.

A silenced voice that rarely speaks,
Just in art or satin sheets.
Sometimes it gets so hard to breathe,
Till I pop a (pen) cap, and then relief...

About the poem:

Stop playing with me 'fore I turn you into a poem

I'm a big fan of Kendrick Lamar, and I really like the flow of 'Rich Spirit', so I tried to emulate it in this poem. This poem describes all of the reasons why I write, with the main reason being stated at the end i.e., to express myself and manage my wellbeing. I'm so glad that I fell in love with writing and music at a young age, I owe these artforms my life, literally. I wonder if it is obvious, but I am basically describing what it's like finding/creating voice as one of the voiceless.

MELANATED MADNESS

Black stoic–
Keep it pumping for the black voice.
Know where I am going–
If I am guided by the black ploy.

Light a joint for the days I find no point.
Black choice is to keep on grinding, stay poised.
I got word for the people that they ex–ploit,
This is your world too. you've got to fight and show it!

Your black is showing,
So, you wash away the Ebonics.
Code–switching is a black child's first language.
The black experience is a magic that's enjoyed in silence.

When black noise
Is to beg for air because you're drowning!
And "Black joy
Should be penalised before they're thriving!"

My fault...
I'm just a black woman – tired of trying.

About the poem:

Melanated madness

This poem is angry, tired, yet determined and hopeful. I am speaking about the unfair targeting of black joy – however that it may manifest. The bastardisation of black noise as just an unreasonable and unwarranted wail. I am speaking about my experience of code-switching and bilingualism, as an uncomfortable practice, especially for someone that values authenticity. A message that I want to be highlighted through this piece is that 'this is your world too'. This is a message to my younger self, other black kids, and anyone else that feels like an alien (regardless of race). One of the reasons I hate racism is because it is built on lies that bully people into ill health (like all forms of prejudice).

As someone stuck between two worlds, I can see how the West destroyed, stole, and adulterated my history, so much so that a lot of European British people are ignorant of their own country's atrocities – much less miseducated immigrants! Sadly, so too are a lot of Africans, since Westernisation dominates the globe, we have been conditioned to believe in our supposed inferiority. Basically, what I am saying is that the West was a bully that started a rumour that they were the coolest kid in school, maybe because they secretly felt that they weren't, who knows. Through various bullying practices, and just downright mean behaviours, the West manage to convince the whole school (the world), that indeed they were the coolest kid in school, which made their worldview the standard to attain. The only world that mattered.

THE
WEST, YOU
DO THE
MOST

The absence of culture
Gives way to blunders,
That turn sincerity—
Into something vulgar.

Why is love between consenting olders—
Involving children and their exposure?
Leave youth alone, you disgusting vultures!
Just a system trapped in deep inertia.

You don't care about equality or equity,
You want to find a way to break all that is unity.
The fact that we have to assign rights to entities,
Speaks volume of the ugly in humanity.

Listen West, your freedom begets access to opportunity,
But my opportunities are still new to me.
That's why I rarely make queerness an identity,
Because there's so much more that means to me.

Like making sure my family eats.

About the poem:

The West, you do the most

A difficult piece, and perhaps led more so by uninformed outrage than a comprehensive viewing of all of the facts. This piece is about the recent trend in all media outlets, regarding merging the LGTBQ+ conversation with the affairs of children. I suspect that it is another distracting tactic by big media and government, but nonetheless, the conversation is fuelled by participating members of the public. Let me just state this, as a queer person of colour, I do not feel represented by the western queer agenda. They had me at marriage rights, and the right to live in peace, and not be killed for being queer, but lost me at allowing children to undergo drastic body modifications and discussing sexualities with 5-year-olds.

I think there is a conversation that needs to be had about what it means to be an ethnic minority queer, like all of the opportunities that are still new to us as 1st or 2nd generation queer immigrants. All of the nuances regarding racism, culture, and queerness, the different experiences of queer folk in different parts of the world, and how this can influence our political perspectives/priorities. I think what I am trying to say is that I feel further victimised by my own group (queer people in the West), as a black queer person, because I do not feel like I have a voice in this conversation and my politics are being underrepresented or misconstrued because I belong to the LGBTQ+.

TWO CAN PLAY THAT GAME

Narrator:
Mammy was a maid,
Used to raise and birth her masters, shame.
And she's still just the same, working 9 to 9 to save—
for a life for all her babes, who rarely see her grace.

Pappy had no name,
Just another pawn with pain.
A stallion that was tamed
To lead itself to early graves.

Brother:
"So, guess what then became,
Of my bitch, and kids unclaimed?
They learned to hate themselves,
While I was stuck up in a cage."

Sister:
"Wait who you calling bitch—
My nigga you need to behave.
I do you, like they do you,
Tell my kids you're just insane."

Narrator:
And as they fought through time and space,
Being distracted and being afraid,
This has always been the master's way,
To make no room to plan for change.

Imagine if they stopped to wonder,
And finally came to another's aid.
That'd be a complete disaster,
If the slave finally realised, they're enslaved...

About the poem:

Two can play at that game

A favourite movie of mine, and a fitting metaphor to describe the tradition of black heteronormative gender roles. Again, I will try not to generalise, so let's keep this commentary within the context of the West, specifically black America in this case, owing to the language within the allegory. See, Rome wasn't built in a day, and it takes two to tango. The contemporary gender-related discourse happening i.e., 'gender wars', is reintroducing implicit or neglected, and arguably counterproductive topics within black spaces. I don't know if this is the same for other races and ethnicities, but it seems, the rise of 'gender wars', has had a regressive effect on the (western) black community, by reinstating conversations about interracial dating, the devaluation and disrespect of black women, and the vilification of black men. I believe that these gender wars are another type of global, nonsensical symptoms of shared trauma through our universal experience of the pandemic and economic collapse.

Yet, the heteronormative black space has taken this opportunity to remind us of opinions which we tried to leave behind in the 90s and 2000s. I just feel like it is hard to take anyone seriously who doesn't take themselves seriously. Moreover, that the traumas in these relationships are not inherent to blackness, nor isolated to those couples, but they are an observable and attributable pattern of behaviours sourced from unknowing ourselves. Side note, I also wrote this as a poem outside of race, and rather, about the relationship between two individuals/groups. In that case, the master is government and big business, and the common man is the enslaved (tell me I'm lying).

While we're down here arguing about what a woman is, whether men should foot the bill, whether privilege exists etc., someone else is having the real important conversations and making the real important decisions about our lives. Instead of fighting each other and finding any reason to invalidate another human experience from fear that it threatens our own, I think we'd be stronger together. But I guess that's the task, the dream, and perhaps just a utopian Marxist fantasy where a collective class consciousness becomes materialised.

REFUGEE

57

I was but a child,
Awakened consciousness, wild.
Born in the South,
Mwana Wevhu and Proud.

It was on my mother's back,
That I felt UK ground.
It was firstly in their words,
That I learned I was brown.

We were homeless, it was bleak,
But never lost just found—
A place of refuge from the heat
As our oppressors frowned.

Let not the diasporans speak,
Without their mother tongue,
To forget your language means
Forget yourself, your sound.

So, if you're really needing free,
And far away from lands you seek,
Culture nurtured me—
The only advice I have to preach.

About the poem:

Refugee

My immigration journey only added to my existential angst, and tendency to think of life as absurd. A lot of who we are is based on the countries we grew up in, but what happens when you've grown up in different countries, and in different counties and therefor different social classes as well? Identity is such a fickle thing, yet foundational to the human experience. No wonder why one of life's biggest questions is: 'who am I', because there isn't an 'I' to find, we're all interconnected (one). Of course, this is my philosophy, and this philosophy comes from the fact that I, myself, am a huge contradiction (aren't we all?). I may write all day about my pro-blackness and all the different ways I am, or have been subjugated by whiteness, but that doesn't negate the white women I've loved and the white friends I've adored in my life.

Equally, it doesn't alleviate my rage towards counterproductive African traditions. What I'm saying is that, in as much as identity is created from experience and DNA, it is not all we are or all that we're destined to be. When we feel lost and confused, by all means, it is healthy to venture deep and get back to the basics of what we embody within this world i.e., DNA and experiences. But for the sake of evolution, spirituality, and connectedness, I believe that being an immigrant taught me that we're more alike than we are different. Unfortunately, the world doesn't function on hippie sentiments, that's why I wrote this poem. This poem is about having to forget yourself to survive, and then having to remember yourself to thrive.

AT LEAST IT'S NOT JAIL OR CRACK

There's a little box in my soul,
That I keep hidden from most.
Made of nothing but gold,
You'd think it's something to hold.

I feel the weight of it and its cold,
Hearing the creatures scream, "Let us go!",
I keep them trapped until I am old,
When I am finally free to just erode.

There's a beast in me that's always growling on the low.
I run so fast towards light because darkness is all I know.
Wearing calmness like a holy cloak so my rage still folds,
I'm nothing to behold, just madness composed.

Thank goodness I am nothing like the places I'm from,
Just a beauty that's disguising the ugliness I've known.
If I ever lose the battle between my darkness and my glow,
Well...at least I will have put up one hell of a show.

About the poem:

At least it's not jail or crack

There's nothing explicitly black about this poem besides the title perhaps. This poem is about being beautiful in an ugly world, being the rose that grew from concrete (Tupac). We all carry hidden woes and have each survived our share of adversity. However, there is a reason that we recognise marginalised and vulnerable people because we logically can observe the disproportionate barriers that they experience in life, which are either naturally or socially constructed. That's why when I think of ethnic minority people, and my own lived experience, there is a reason why 'black pride' is a thing. Why 'gay pride', 'crip pride', 'femme pride' etc., are all things that need to continue existing.

These are terms that declare survival and triumph, a refusal to be silenced or erased in a world that is actively trying to destroy or subjugate you. This poem is about living through hell and wearing it well, except, don't be fooled to think we don't have burns and scars to show for it. Every survivor/warrior has battle scars. These could be anything from maladaptive behaviours like substance abuse (hey, that's me!) to personality disorders. Nevertheless, these people mask very well, so much so that some of them don't know how to recognise their own pain. Also, what happens when the pain becomes too much to bear? Which happens more often than we'd like to admit. That's where the real tragedy lies, in the premature demise of potential, and within the surrendering of willpower. I guess the title of this poem is an alternative phrasing to 'it could have been worse', but how worse does it have to get? (Blowing in the wind by Bob Dylan).

FREEDOM

Hear me gush
About dreams and fears in us.
We're just alike, we come from mud,
My family drenched in blood.

Are we victims or the villains?
When we're both, after all that we've been given.
Sometimes this life has got me thinking,
We got no choice, it's all been written,
We got no voice, it's all cognition,
So, think in scripture, your word's religion.

Forever is a day, dazed with an ache,
Trapped in the moments of dreaded heartbreak.
We're a believer's rage, after listening to the fakes,
No, we don't plan on staying, in this land of poisonous
snakes.

About the poem:

Freedom

One of my life goals is to achieve 'freedom' as I've defined it. For as long as I could remember, I've never liked being told what to do if it felt wrong, nonsensical, or unclear. I've always been keen to follow – only if I am following the highest and/or shared good, for which, there is very little of that going on in our world, so one might be forced to pave their own path. Freedom to me, is an enabler to self-actualisation within the pursuit of eudaimonia. I believe that we are at our best when we're allowed to choose who we want to be. I don't thrive under authoritarian rule, and I want more than patriarchy, provides e.g., love, intimacy, compassion, nurturing, time/patience. This poem is about, and for anybody who is tired of Earth (Aliah Sheffield), or at least the lies we tell each other. This poem is for anyone that rejects the societal chains that are normalised and so frequently passed down in generations.

DON'T

DREAD

THESE

LOCS

I'm loc'd and loaded,
I've got all my treasures soaked and woven,
In these matted strands, which are tinted golden,
To represent a dream unbroken.

I'm black beauty and its scrutiny, Jesse Owens.
These ropes are truths which mark our progress.
I dip my roots in castor lotions,
To nurse a history of crossing oceans.

This kink harbours strength awoken,
Like Samson's mane, a walking poem.
But to think my charm could cause commotion,
With fingers in my hair, I'm not your token!

See, me and my hair, we've got herstory,
Let us be – we don't want to have to cut and weave.
Dodging hate and animosity,
I wear my pride, you can tell them fuck their policies!

About the poem:
Don't dread these locs

I think the fact that 'black hair' is a conversation on its own is fascinating. Like, there is a whole history of black hair in terms of African tribal fashion versus black hair as pillow stuffing for enslavers or maps to freedom for the enslaved. That's why I wrote this poem, because of the symbolism of black hair and as the poem states, the commotion it has caused on this planet throughout history. I have dreadlocks because (1) I've always thought they're cool since a child, (2) it's a protective and practical style, given that I am disabled and cannot do my own hair, (3) and it was a spiritual choice at the age of 20. None of these reasons are because I am black, and I do not think that the hairstyle should be gatekept by black people (anymore). In the past, I wanted to gatekeep the style simply because of the way white society treated me versus a white person wearing dreadlocks.

I saw white people with dreadlocks in professional positions way before it was acceptable for black people to have them, unlike nowadays where these stigmas are slowly disappearing. Back in my day, black kids, especially in rural England, couldn't go to school with anything more than a short, combed afro. Anything more than that, we got letters sent home to our parents, whilst our white peers got 'isolation' for having pink hair, shaved sides, and piercings. That's why I wanted to gatekeep the hairstyle, as retaliation for the double standards in white culture, and I wonder if that's why other people of colour have a problem with white people appropriating their worlds. For me, it's not because you're white, it's because the world is already yours and you want the little that I've got. Further, I don't get to be myself in your spaces, but you get to be me, how does that work?

This poem is a rant if anything, a rebellious declaration I had to pen down in my early 20s. It's an old poem but it still speaks to me. PS, me and my hair are 7 years going/growing strong!

AMBITION: THE CURE OR THE POISON

Mama I'm scared...
They don't know about the hurt.
I'm afraid they are going to hate me
Because I'm so hungry to be first.

They don't understand
That I've been nothing since birth,
When insignificance stained my DNA
Like a curse.

If only I could send my message
In one verse,
I'd put my two cents
Into society's purse,
And tell her she's a groupie
For rich, old, white, straight, men from church.

About the poem:

Ambition: the cure or the poison

You can view this piece through the lenses of most people. (1) I am writing about the 'crabs in a bucket' mentality that plagues black communities and families, (2) I am writing about being disabled and underestimated, (3) I am writing about trying to achieve equity as a black minority in the West. One day, the question suddenly struck me: is ambition the cure or the poison? We like to promote and admire ambitious people but is ambition as healthy as everyone suggests?

This was one of the first steps towards my philosophy regarding ambition and addiction being both sides of the same coin, as I am growing to view self-development and self-destruction as cousins, if not siblings. This is probably not an original thought, but it is certainly one I've had through my lived experience as an ambitious substance abuser. I put it to you, dear reader, is ambition a cure or a poison? Considering all that happens to people and what people do in the name of ambitious endeavours. Do the ends really justify the means? Is it really worth the chase or are we just running away (in another direction from self-destruction), from dealing with our pain properly.

TOUGH LOVE

...That's some black mothers for you—
No time for cuddles.
But they'll really die for you,
That's why they hustle.

About the poem:

Tough Love

A short one about my thoughts on some black mothers' love language. Back to black women being valued for their labour, so I suppose our black mothers learn to love us through acts of service, whilst potentially neglecting other crucial childhood needs. But of course, she is one person, and the world already demands too much of her without seeing her at all. The least that I can do as her child, is recognise her exponential efforts.

CYPHER

It's not written in the books for me,
So, I built my own stage – making Herstory,
But why am I always on the edge of defeat?
Popping pills, cowardice tastes sweet to me.

'Cos a doobie calms the nerves but it's killing me,
So, I'm choking on my pride, avoiding healing me.
But I do be on my grind, so it's hard to sleep,
When I'm dreaming about the things we could get to see.

About the poem:

Cypher

This is my homage to hip hop rap culture, a short piece that if I had the confidence and access, I'd rap in a cypher! Every word that is written is true and felt.

KILL THEM BEFORE THEY GROW

If your soul is to be devoured,
It's through turning pain into power.
"I cannot breathe" ...within this hour,
As my brothers fall like towers.

They see monsters, I see flowers,
That grow from concrete, never cowered.
And there's no strength like ours
As we rise from shame – empowered.

With our mothers crying louder,
You keep quiet, as you tend to doubt her.
A yearning for justice as we scour,
On this desolate land of cowards.

About the poem:

Kill them before they grow

Inspired by Bob Marley's lyrics, I wrote this poem during the Black Lives Matter and George Floyd incident. I don't deny that media has a way of fuelling certain discourse to increase the divide between people in society, and that most media content is rage bating nowadays. Still, I don't know about other people, but the reason I get upset during moments when another black/brown person is killed (whether in America or Britain), or when I support groups like BLM (before the scandals), it's because it's one of a few moments in my life that part of my pain is televised for the world to see. Yes, of course, I am not the one who was shot dead, but I've had so many explicit and implicit experiences of racial violence that I might as well have been. You die many deaths before they actually kill you. That's why I wrote this poem, because my heart was breaking, and I was experiencing a form of PTSD from my own race-related trauma.

BLACK
POWER(LESSNESS)

Durags and Bonnets
Like head wraps on prophets.
Ancestors in chains,
Now we keep ours in closets.

The new slave engaged
to promiscuous profits,
Hoping consumption
heals all that is broken.

In truth it reveals all the words left unspoken,
Like how to exist with these hearts that are frozen.
We buy or we envy what we think is golden,
Trying to replace what we think was stolen.

Some roll up their pain
And smoke it for a moment,
Just waiting for change
While they're too scared to own it.

Some live on just change,
There's no cap on their pockets,
Buying and exchanging
Everything we concocted.

When what's fed to you has been lies and just vomit,
It's not surprise that you grew up to be toxic.
The new chains imposed through cognitive sockets,
But it's mind over matter – our lineage posits.

About the poem:

Black power(lessness)

Back to radical accountability. This poem is about the juxtaposing reality of how we live our lives now compared to our black ancestors. Here is another moment that I am shining the spotlight on our own communal behaviours, our norms and values, the things we praise and the things we neglect to consider. Much like my other poem 'African child', this poem is about taking accountability of maladaptive and counterintuitive behaviours, whilst exercising compassion by recognising black history. Basically, this life and the role you have to play is not your fault, but it is your fault how you choose to play it.

FOR GHETTO KIDS

Kings and Queens don't fall, they just reign,
As I watch these kids rise up – amidst pain.
Not all heroes fly or wear capes,
With billions left without homes; just graves.

Inspired by the dark and the strange,
With tears in my eyes and poison in the veins.
Learned to live a lie so that we can maintain,
That's a relatable plight, that poor-kids proclaim.

I can never turn a blind eye, from whence my mother came,
To think she was yay high, fighting for her name.
In a world that only spotlights the rich or insane,
We're leaving little kids dry, without a drop of hope or change.

I pray that ghetto birds fly – not just copper planes,
and I pray they always stay bright, in the darkness that we make.
Keep on smiling with your heads high, you remind us that we're brave,
That human nature is to take flight, and not be grounded by our chains.

About the poem:

For Ghetto Kids

I've been a ghetto kid / inner city kid, and I wasn't the first or the only one in my family. I've always found the concept of a ghetto very poetic and a good representation of modernity. Ghettos everywhere will show you who mankind is, and not who we claim to be. It will show you our carelessness, disdain for self and other, hypocrisy, greed, and so forth. Equally, and within that manmade depravity, it will show you the resilience, if not divinity of mankind. Within this humanmade ugliness, sprouts a spectrum of humanmade beauty. It's almost conflicting for me, because I do not want ghettos to exist, but there is so much beauty and philosophy in ghettos that would be a shame to lose for mankind. Anyway, this is a poem for children in any ghetto: I am rooting for you more than you know. We all are (former ghetto kids).

SAVE ME

I'll tell you why I gave up on love,
Right before I resist the temptation to touch—
A bottle of spirits, a clover of luck,
A job to finish, a hit if I must.

Talking 'bout love is doing too much,
I can barely risk giving some trust,
When growing up was a little bit rough,
Cause I did my best just to feel I'm enough.

See, my King and Queen were getting uncuffed:
Nuclear family about to combust.
I saw the worst. The eldest. A leader of none.
He saw me hurt, I'm guilty – for what he's become.

I did it first, a pill on my tongue.
Unquenchable thirst, He drinks till he's numb.
'These siblings are smart but they're equally dumb',
Since Daddy said a beer will keep you from glum—

And Mama never knew how to have fun,
So, imbalanced scales keep me ready to jump.
Traumatic memories – I cannot outrun.
Traumatic memories – I smoke till it's crumbs.

But I've had the good, the bad, the moon, and the sun.
When I've seen the light, the dark, the gloom and the scum.
I know it's right, to never get tired, so we overcome,
But just for tonight, I beg you be quiet...this love shit's for chumps.

About the poem:

Save me

This is a poem about my childhood and how I come from a broken home. Again, I don't think being a child of divorcees is inherent to blackness but it sure is a common pattern! Don't get me wrong, it's not the divorce that mattered (to me anyway), it was the neglect that I experienced thereafter. And a bit prior, to be honest. Anyway, this poem also describes what happens when you're the eldest and have siblings who witness your own trauma: that they can learn it too. Pain gets passed down like hand-me-downs in those situations. Importantly, this is not an opportunity for weirdos to say 'see, tHeY alL cOmE fRoM BroKEN HoMES', or whatever nonsense, but it is an opportunity to discuss the shared experiences we have as black minorities e.g., the reasons for the divorces and how both parents fail their children as a result of not getting a divorce or getting one and failing further after that.

Black love, another conversation that needs to be had, properly – outside of gender wars. What I saw of black love, from the two people that were supposed to model it for me, ruined my hopes of finding love or wanting children. This is something that I've noticed and now have to unlearn and heal from, if I am ever to be whole and accept love into my life again. A few artists have touched on this topic, 'Your House' by Hopsin, 'Boo Boo the fool' by Aliah Sheffield, and 'Hereditary' by JID, just to name a few. As previously mentioned by other prominent black thinkers, the black home is where we need to start. It's not the separation that is the problem, because people are people and life happens, it's how we fail the individuals that we supposedly promised to commit to, and those we birthed/sired.

CYPHER 2

I was the type of kid that couldn't be told what I was meant for,
Always had potential but they saw nothing but flaws.
Self-hating got me self-medicating till my guts sore.
But maturing got me seeing, I'm a gorgeous beast like Centaur.

They ignore our pleas now hear them turn (in)to uproar,
I summon freaks – be bold not meek,
And we don't need your applause.
We been winning battles since before your civil rights laws,
We don't need permission just to eat when we've got jaws.

Cause with every door they closed,
I was smashing windows.
And with every dream they broke,
I still pictured it like Kenko.

I feel it in my mental,
I'm on the edge or on a threshold.
And you'll never see my knees fold,
But you can watch me light my green
And shine, just like Emerald.

About the poem:

Cypher 2

The sequel to my homage to hip hop rap. A motivational piece about being a rebel with a cause, about rising time after time (Dr. Angelou), about shining regardless.

A KING IN PLATO'S CAVE

We cornered him to a cave,
Screaming hate and enraged.
Forced him to eat away his faith,
Just to emerge broken and scathed.

With our pitchforks and flames
We burned away his name(s).
Then why do we stand in shock,
When we're the ones to blame?

Still, what a cowardly lion to feel so unsafe,
When even the sheep know they're doomed, yet remain unfazed.
Now hypnotised by false truths, from denial untamed,
Which makes me wonder, if that's all it takes to keep a King in chains?

About the poem:

A King in Plato's Cave

This poem is about a lost black boy. It describes the various ways that I've seen black boys dehumanised, and emasculated, e.g., robbed of name and status, which is what maketh a man in this world. I've watched how black boys are vilified, even when they're the kindest and softest souls. How they're often the target of scrutiny even when they're blameless or get worser punishments for trying to defend themselves. I watched for 20 years, to be exact, as I watched my brothers/peers grow up. Be that as it may, that's not enough to give up on yourself and your glory. Even people who are deemed immutably wrong, e.g., the disabled, still dare to dream and gamble against the odds. They still fight for self and do not yield into self-hate. That's why I ask, dear black boy, is that all it takes to make you give up on life?

Do better, Kings.

Growing up in Inner City London:

Tales from my childhood.

1996

I grew up all over the place,
You could say my roots are all over the place.
I've got flashbacks of the orange dawn that shines in the African morn.
My mother tongue is poetry alone,
I could never forget home.

Then when I was five
Me and my mum flew for miles.
She ventured for a 'cure' for her child,
I guess acceptance takes a while.

See, immigration is just a joke to a child,
I used to wonder why mama never smiled,
Yet I could hear her stomach growl,
Washing me in the sink; trying to find a way out.

She also had to leave my baby brothers,
That year, she used to panic – on the phone all different hours.
She's a Queen, I give her power,
Left her life to give us ours.

I spent a year homeless with my mother,
That's a bond like no other.
I've watched her rise and crawl from the gutters.

Oh yeah, shout out to my father.

2003

I always say London holds a special place in my heart,
There's a realness in these streets that sets us apart.
I'm not talking about crumpets and tea,
Man, we struggled to eat.

And my mother was 'that' hood mother,
The type you could never take her pride from her,
Teaching her kids: 'you better do right and act proper'.

We used to watch TV with rats at our feet,
The winters were better because the roaches would flee.
2 bedrooms, 3 kids, so you know it was a squeeze,
But even with ghetto birds surveying the scene,
As kids we played out, filled with nothing but glee.

Friendly encounters with criminals and fiends,
Because children are innocent – they just see human beings.

'What's your name, what's your street?'
A bunch of children circled me.
I said my area code and I heard some kiss their teeth,
Whilst others cheered and set me free.

Because gang initiation's just a breeze,
Lack of contemplation, education,
Makes recruitment move with ease.
We had nothing to copy but bravado from the monsters that we see,
With the lack of guidance that we seek.

And so, we watched our friends bleed,
Fathers abandon seeds,
The degradation of Queens,
With burning family trees.

That's why we had to go,
Mama said skid row is a place her children shouldn't ever have to know.

Fin.

Author

A Zimbabwean born, Black British artist and researcher, Gamuchirai has Spinal Muscular Atrophy-type 2, and so, her life's work mainly centres around existentialism and her disabled lived experience, regarding disability as a profoundly enigmatic yet universalising phenomena. Her earliest literary works include a play called: The Girl in a Wheelchair, which she wrote and directed in primary school (2005), and two self-published chapbooks in secondary school called: Heartfelt poems (2009), and: A Share of Thoughts (2011).

"My name means embrace/accept in simple terms, which is ironic and poetic in itself. And before we let ableism win the day, no — I was named before they knew I'd be a magnificent beast.

However, I live up to my name in encouraging people to embrace the absurd (Camus), that is, me, you, us, we. Living authentically, optimally, and practicing goodness for goodness' sake. Remember, nobody gets out alive, and this is not a dress rehearsal so take yourself and your life seriously."

Gamuchirai Karen Mutsatsa